37 Seconds to Impact

7 Powerful Ways to Impact Your Life

Dedicated to my Grandmother

Carrie Bell Edwards

37 Seconds to Impact

7 Powerful Ways to Impact Your Life

Terrell G. Edwards

Since 2007

West Columbia   Houston   Longview   Austin
New York City

Acknowledgments

"37 Seconds to Impact" marks the 1st edition of the series of books which God has allowed me to write in order to speak life into people and their situations. It is actually the 2nd volume in the trio of books which the Lord is allowing me to leave in my legacy of motivation. It's taken all this year to pray, meditate and also allow him to prepare my soul for the mission of transforming myself into his image and equipping me to change lives.

There have been times when I wanted to write the book, get fame for myself, be recognized and brag about writing two books and separating myself from the average things I felt others did. So it's taken all of the first 11 months of 2016, and now I wake up at 5:17 am on December 1 to compile what God has given to me.

It is important to move in God's timing. This has made all the difference. You allow God to create a work through you, and the desire is to thank all those who pushed you forward along the way, gave some insight, opened their hearts to listen, or showed their concern.

You'll never remember to thank everyone; it's impossible, because the very time you make the list, you'll see someone you missed at the store. I'll just do my best, and let God build the thank you list. In my 1st book I thanked everyone, I mean everyone; maybe even 300 people. It's better to include them, even if they did little to nothing than to omit them and hear their mouth. In this book, I wanted to thank 37 people who were crucial in my life and development.

First thanks goes to my maternal grandmother, **Carrie Bell Edwards**, who disciplined me, watched me when I was sick at home from school, fed me, protected me and guided me toward my goals. She was invaluable to me ,because her talking to me as I was leaving or preparing to leave out and go into the world set the stage for me get fine tuning. Most of my essentials I got from my mother, while she was running trying to make ends meet.

My grandmother gave me one on one conversation and great tools that I listened to, since I knew I needed all the strategies to make it in this competitive world. She made me feel important for not only having a desire for me to excel in life, but also to speak life into others.

I thank my family for being the foundational structure in which I could grow and teach others: my wife, **Sheila**; kids: **Shundra, Terrell, Jr. and Andrew.**

I thank my mother, **Johnnie Faye Edwards** for endless amount of parental love and education. Thanks to my maternal grandfather, **Johnny Woodson Edwards** for teaching me work ethics, compassion for those disabled, and how to be a go-getter.

Thanks to my father, **Thomas Humphrey**, who was never there for me, but what he taught me in the last 10 years has provided deeper insight about the realities of life.

Thanks to my 3 brothers: Gary, Shawn and Stephen for your foundational presence. Thanks to all my Aunts and Uncles: Ollistine, Willie, Merilyn, Barbara, Dennis, Marshall, Karen, Greg, Annette, Carolyn, and Anissa.

Thanks to all my cousins for their hugs, words, joy, from Sharone to Cheryl to Kara to Kameron to Kendra to Verlondra and Verlencia and Vernon and Sandy and Sandra, Bessie, Michael, Kevin and Kayle.

Thanks to all the good Bruhz of Omega Psi Phi Fraternity, Inc. (Longview Eta Chi Chapter) the Mighty Mother Theta and Nu Iota chapters for giving me the

foundation I needed in manhood, scholarship, perseverance and uplift.

Especially brothers: **Billy Goffney**, **Joe Pierce**, Chris Watson, Jeremy McCray ,**David Faggett**, Robbie Cox, Luther Freeman, Robert Knox, Louis Tennison Jr ,Aubrey Brazile,Johnny Hamilton, Eugene Beavers and other brothers who supported me in my process and journey, I'll thank you in person. Thanks to all the Delta sisters who spoke a pleasant word: Kasha, Cheteva, Kim and others

I thank my friends and associates for their guidance: Ray Crumley, Alvin Harvey, Raymond Hicks, Mandel

Stoker, Hershel Lomax, Kenneth Walker, Garlene Horton, Evelyn, and Jell Williams.

Thanks to all my Cali cousins: Vincent, Pat, Rene, Essie, Donnaise, and Trey.

Thanks to my **Charlie Brown 1st grade crew**: **William, Davylon, Georgia, and Sharmarion** for the beginning.

Thanks to my poetic friends: Princess, Latifah, Chandra, Sleepy, Emmitt, Les, Datonya, Joshua and Christina.

Appreciations to Lakeicha and her mother, Pokie for realness and the long talks we had and sometimes still have.

Thanks to those who gave me acting opportunities and chances to present my skills: E'Tian, Earl Bonner, Angela, Tonika, Endya, Jamye, Princess and Patricia Pamplin.

Thanks to the Longview NAACP members for preparing me and believing in me.

Special appreciations to Michele, for her biblical insight, support, sincerity; and Carolyn for her perspective.

I honor the life of my classmate, Douglas Williamson, who came from Houston to my book signing and gave inspiration for this book, "37 Seconds to Impact.

I also thank **Michael Ramsey** for his spiritual positivity and quotes as, Christ gave his all for us, and all God wants is for us to be happy in him. I also thank life guards: **Robert Sweeney**, Malori, and all the Paula Jones Recreation center members who've made my job a great experience for speaking life into people.

Poolside Chat

While working at the recreation center, I decided to stroll and check on things. I went to the pool area and saw the lifeguard, **Robert** talking with a swimmer. I asked them both what you would say to someone in 37 seconds ,if they were facing extreme difficulties in their life. The swimmer answered, "I'd pray for them and Robert said, **"I'd tell them I love them"**. I smiled and told them that I never thought of those answers. It came to me that sometimes you just rub their shoulder or grab their hand, say **"I love and I'm praying for you"**! That's enough!

Most importantly, I thank God for the journey he's allowing me to see and hope he's allowing me to present to others.

Symbolism

of

37 Seconds to Impact

P eople will ask and have asked me about the

meaning and significance of my 2nd book,*" 37 Seconds of Power*". I'll simply answer them with this story, which will set the tone for this journey.

My initial purpose was to write this book, *"37 seconds to Impact"* in 2017, and in 2016 write a motivational play , *"the Best in Me"*, into a 2nd book .

God changes the order and steps of life, and as we encounter different people and go through the seasons he has for us; we gotta accept his direction. So in December, 2016, through advice from friends; I changed the name of my book to *"37 Seconds to Impact"*.

In 2016, the country and the community had been bombarded with those tiring political elections, and the people were hurting and you'd see it in their living. Angela Lilly was putting on a comedy production, and I was cast as a clown; so I went inside this 2nd hand store near CC's pizza and found some size 14 shoes that I could paint, for $ 4.00.

The employees were nice and helpful, and as I walked out, I saw a display of bluish t-shirts with something very strange on them. The words, **"Free People"**, and at the bottom a scripture, Luke 4:18. I didn't initially see the scripture, just the big words, **Free People, Free People.**

I was puzzled, because I never saw such a shirt, and I asked the clerk, what the phrase meant. She said it dealt with the world being caught up in bondage, shackles and confusion and how Christ wants us to have abundant life. People bound by pressures of life, are hindered and handicapped from planting the seeds of the gospel and speaking life into people who so need it. So I returned a week later and bought 2 shirts, 1 for me and 1 for my wife.

I plant seeds by telling people about scriptures, studying them, and memorizing them for power and encouragement to others. Share this with someone today.

This scripture, Luke 4:18 will help people move from just surviving in life to living the life Christ desires for us abundantly.

Luke 4:18

King James Version (KJV)

18 The Spirit of the Lord is upon me, because he hath anointed me to preach the gospel to the poor; he hath sent me to heal the brokenhearted, to preach deliverance to the captives, and recovering of sight to the blind, to set at liberty them that are bruised,

Definitions

Symbolism.....the use of symbols to represent ideas or qualities.

Surviving.....continue to just or exist, possibly day by day in spite of danger or hardship

Living....pursuit of a lifestyle, living with a truth plan of living, possibly abundantly

Luke 4:18....the spirit of the Lord is upon me.....

2 Timothy 3: 1-7.....This know also, that in the last days perilous times shall come.....

Free people........symbolized by Luke 4:18, connected with Christ and not letting earthly shackles trap you in bondage.

37 ....*Signifies* independence, freedom

37 seconds...what if you had 37 seconds to encourage and empower someone? What would your interaction be?

Speak life.......encourage someone, plant a seed for life growth

Proverbs 18:21....the tongue has the power of life and death

Table of Contents
37 Seconds to Impact

Introduction...."Androcles and the Lion"

The Significance of "37"

Chapter 1 ...Alcoholism/ Drug Addiction

Chapter 2...Terminal Illness / Cancer

Chapter 3......... Death / the End?

Chapter 4 ....37 Points of Impact

Chapter 5....Depression

Chapter 6....Divorce

Chapter 7....Emotional /Mental Problems

Chapter 8.... Unemployment

Chapter 9..... The Homeless

Chapter 10....Suicide

Chapter 11....Millennial Mania

Chapter 12....Inspirational Poetry

Chapter 13...Motivational short stories

Chapter 14... Health

Chapter 15....Questions and Answers

Chapter 16...37 Seconds response

Chapter 17.....Closing Thought and card

Inspirational Poetry Corner

A. I See Masks

B. The Waiting Room

C. Abundant Life

D. In Da 17

E. Faded White Picket Fences

F. Snakes Don't Hiss No More

G. You Can't Hear Cause You Got That Roach in Your Ear

H. Think Outside the Box

Motivational Short Stories

H. God Is Using You for Good

I. Life is Short

J. I'm 6' 5"

K.. 288 and Almeda/ Houston

L.. Evolution of a Dream

M. Free People

N. 2nd Chances

O. Surprise Hug

P. Memorial to Rene

20

Androcles and the Lion

THIS STORY takes place in Rome, where a Greek slave named Androcles escaped from his master and fled into the forest. There he wandered for a long time until he was weary and well-nigh spent with hunger and despair. Just then he heard a lion near him moaning and groaning and at times roaring terribly. Tired as he was, Androcles rose up and rushed away, as he thought, from the lion; but as he made his way through the bushes he stumbled over the root of a tree and fell down lamed. When he tried to get up, there he saw the lion coming towards him, limping on three feet and holding his forepaw in front of him.

Poor Androcles was in despair; he had no strength to rise and run away, and there was the lion coming upon him. But when the great beast came up to him instead of attacking him it

kept on moaning and groaning and looking at Androcles, who saw that the lion was holding out his right paw, which was covered with blood and much swollen.

Looking more closely at it, Androcles saw a great big thorn pressed into the paw, which was the cause of all the lion's trouble. Plucking up courage he seized hold of the thorn and drew it out of the lion's paw, who roared with pain when the thorn came out, but soon after found such relief from it that he fawned upon Androcles and showed, in every way that he knew, to whom he owed the relief. Instead of eating him up, he brought him a young deer that he had slain, and Androcles managed to make a meal from it. For some time the lion continued to bring the game he had killed to Androcles, who became quite fond of the huge beast.

But one day a number of soldiers came marching through the forest and found Androcles. As he could not explain what he was doing, they took him prisoner and brought him back to the town from which he had fled. Here his master soon found him and brought him before the authorities. Soon Androcles was condemned to death for fleeing from his master. Now it used to be the custom to throw murderers and other criminals to the lions in a huge circus, so that while the criminals were punished the public could enjoy the spectacle of a combat between them and the wild beasts.

So Androcles was condemned to be thrown to the lions, and on the appointed day he was led forth into the Arena and left there alone with only a spear to protect him from the lion. The Emperor was in the royal box that day and gave the signal for the lion to come out and attack Androcles. But when it came out of its cage and got near Androcles, what do you think it did? Instead of jumping upon him, it fawned upon him and stroked him with its paw and made no attempt to do him any harm.

It was of course the lion which Androcles had met in the forest. The Emperor, surprised at seeing such a strange behavior in so cruel a beast, summoned Androcles to him and asked him how it happened that this particular lion had lost all its cruelty of disposition. So

Androcles told the Emperor all that had happened to him and how the lion was showing its gratitude for his having relieved it of the thorn.

Thereupon the Emperor pardoned Androcles and ordered his master to set him free, while the lion was taken back into the forest and let loose to enjoy liberty once more.

37 Seconds of Impact
Alcoholism /Drug Addiction
Chapter 1

Broken families, kids left in turmoil, DWI's, DUI's,

Health problems, fatal accidents seemingly injuring innocent people, and underage drinking, are all attributed to alcohol and alcoholism.

Drunk driving, assaults, violence, kids with behavioral development, and learning disabilities are also connected with alcoholism.

Kids with deficits in their behavior, development or learning and abuse, assaults and violence.

We all have that cousin, friend, brother, father, sister, uncle, and/ or neighbor who just can't seem to deal with alcohol in a safe way. It's not a subject that I have to point a finger

at toward anyone, but it is important enough of a subject to know it needs to be included in the arena of my book.

It' sad, disturbing and disheartening to know that people are endangering the hopes and dreams of themselves, kids and the community with poor decisions and control. I had to offer encouragement, a plan, some benefit to free people of this dangerous drug: alcohol.

What is Alcoholism?

So how do you help an alcoholic?

1. **Be honest**
Be open and honest and tell them you're worried about their behavior and be supportive in a loving way

2. ***Include others who care***, so they trust in the intervention.
3. **Rehearse the plan,** use caring, but positive statements and stress their value
4. ***Pick a good time and place*** to talk.
5. Ensure that the individual is sober, the location is private and interruption free.
6. ***Commit to*** **change**, not settling for vague plans and talk

7. **Stay on Track**

8. **Don't become Codependent** but being supportive and remember that becoming emotional won't help.

9. **Get help for you**
10. **Stay Informed and research**
11. **AAA al_Anon**
12. **SAMha........Substance Abuse and Mental Health Administration**

Do I drink? Yes, I do. Why? Probably because the sweet wine has a taste I really find delicious and I'm learning that it relaxes me and removes in my mind, any inhibitions; so I can relax. People take this too the extreme.

Some will not attend a party unless it's permissible to have alcohol of various types.

I've had parties in my younger years of 15-16 and had much alcohol, which was legal, but could have really cause extremes problems for my parents. I was trying to fit in and be cool, but this was truly not the way. I had yet to learn that people need to love you for you. Beer commercials, I've seen them all my life especially during sporting events. I've been to parties with plenty of liquor, we've had beer and vodka in my house and

really for the longest I never drank. I just didn't feel it was me.

So in this chapter we'll deal with: should you drink, who are the drinkers, what can we do to help the alcoholic, and what does the bible say about drinking?

Gonna be interesting, but most importantly beneficial. I hope you enjoy and share with anyone who needs it.

You probably wonder who is an alcoholic. That is a point we need to begin with. I've researched drinking, spent time with drinkers, and talked to those who indulge.

There exists 4 types of drinkers in my scheme and first we need to know that a basic drink is

A 12 oz. beer, 5 oz. glass of wine, or a mixed drink with 1.5 oz. of liquor.

You'll be surprised to know the types of drinkers.

1st type The Abstainer (low level)

The first type of drinker is the person who doesn't actually drink at all or at a level that is so slight or infrequent that he is at the base O level. He might take a drink once every 3-4 months for a special occasion, but at almost all costs refuses for whatever reason.

2nd type   The Social Drinker

He drinks in small amounts but probably every week yet he has strict boundaries, and he will not cross them. He will drink 1-5 days a week but knows the point in which he or she gets tired or buzzed and immediately back off. They are also in the low risk category.

One in this group might use an extra amount of alcohol for sleep or medical need.

3rd Alcohol abuser or binger

This individual drinks in large amounts as 4 or 5 drinks or more at one sitting is common and it leads to social problems.

His drinking pattern is common and often leads to social problems. This drinker has few boundaries, gets energized after 5 drinks and feels in control, but we know he's probably not. He wants to reach the mountaintop and often has different biological and psychological experiences from ingesting in large amounts.

4th type The Alcoholic

This drinker is dependent on alcohol and is in the high risk category. He consumes often and in great amounts and experiences loss of control and behavior changes at this

Point. If they drink more than they've planned and exhibit work, home, family life, or health issues; then their drinking makes them alcohol dependent. It depends on what happens when they drink; not solely how often or how much. It may be simple to distinguish the low risk drinkers from the high risk, but the highest 2 categories can be similar.

It's also important to know high risk drinkers put themselves in greater risks of DUI, fights, employment problems, family or relationship problems, and health issues.

What does the bible say?

The Old Testament gives numerous examples of strong drink being forbidden. Proverbs is full of warnings against indulging in wine and strong drink, as it refers to wine being
a mocker. Wine mocks those who use it and rewards them with woe, strife, and wounds without cause.

Proverbs 20:1 21:17 23:29

Wine bites like a snake and poisons minds. Paul did suggest to Timothy to use a little wine for his stomach sake, but some consider that unfermented wine. It was important and is important for people (Christians) be of sound mind to reach others and be examples, our bodies are temples and we need ultimate discretion.

Chapter 2

It's a problem which is destroying families and putting financial pressure, stress and strain on American lives. Cancer can range from breast cancer, lung cancer, brain cancer, prostrate cancer, to 20 other types of cancer which are crippling people's health.

I have experienced the scare and fear of cancer as a 14 year old in high school, where I told my mother about a lump in my breast and then a year later another. My mother quickly had the lumps removed and tested and from those 40 years ago, I've been fine and blessed to be clear at this point.

From my 30 years teaching I've had friends who suffered from breast cancer, lung cancer, throat cancer, and other cancerous forms as

Lupus, Aids, and it's often a pattern of fear and gloom. One thing I've noticed is that many times the individual goes into a shell and becomes a hermit. You hear rumors about the person and how they're struggling, been in the hospital, can't go to work and their loss of income. Eventually there comes a point when people give up on them and make excuses for not standing with them in their fight.

I've been one of those in the past who didn't want to visit you in the hospital, visit you at your home or get to close to you. I either felt I was going to be next or I was afraid of the emotional love and attachment that was going to drain me. Maybe it was the fear that it could be me one day.

This has been my pattern until about 1 year ago.

Brother Willie Marshall, the minister at Harrison St. Church of Christ invited me to a bible study they were beginning on the first Wednesday of the month. They were to be studying, "You'll get through this" by Max Lucado.

He made a statement and said, "If you'll participate in this bible

study you can have a book, but if not just use this book when you're here".

He said, the book would benefit us by giving us power to speak life into people and change some atmospheres in their life with joy.

At this time a fellow worker was battling cancer, and I wanted to use these concepts to help her in her battle. I also wanted strength to be able to use the power of encouragement for those hurting and struggling. The power quote that this book stressed was that no matter what your problem or tragedy is …..

You'll get through this

It won't be painless and it won't be quick

But God will use this mess for good.
But in the meantime

Don't be foolish or naïve

But don't despair either

With God's help you'll get through this.

I will never understand cancer, and maybe I don't need to. I do need to be prepared to fortify people's hearts and allow them to fear God and have no fear of these trials of life.

Cancer ....

So What Do You Do When a Friend or Loved One Has Cancer?

It's one of the biggest questions and it will be reoccurring in my book, but we will keep it simple and genuine. The first reaction is to be amazed and want to do something, if anything. The problem is when we know the problem, but not how to respond to it. We often mess it up. So is the answer a call, a gift, a visit, spreading it to others or asking God for direction? I hope to provide some insight, because the response to this incident can greatly get someone through their fight. I can say this, be genuine, prayerful and hopeful in whatever you decide to do.

1. Ask before you go run up to their house. Always remember that there may be 100 other people who just heard and will try to visit you. Call, email, or text them to be sure they're desiring visits and especially your visit. If they agree, consider your time visiting, because you don't know what they're going through. Shorter and more powerful is often more beneficial and ask if

you can return in the near future. Bring a plant, card, gift, food or something when you come in and don't give the presence of being nosey and unconcerned. People can see through that.

2. Listen...show your empathy, don't be asking all kinds of questions. Listen, you'll be surprised at the benefits you'll provide.

3. Offer to do some some basic errands, tasks, things they need to get done, if you can help with those. Don't corner them into agreeing, just let the flow dictate your heart.

4. Take the clues that your friend gives you, don't go in your own direction. Respond to the clues and respond positively.

5. If you bring gifts or food consider their family and consider what your friend can eat and gift cards might be a more suitable option.

6. Don't group all cancer illnesses together. They are distinct. Don't say how you know someone has that cancer and never survived.

7. Be considerate in your gifts and make it motivational always and feel free to include others in the support.

Support the family and their caregivers; this is often a greater asset than bombarding the patient.
8. Continue to encourage through their fight. Spread out and communicate the support with her job, church or neighbors with the friend's permission.
9. Hug and listen and hug

What the Bible Says About Cancer

Man put himself in the position for calamity. While on earth Jesus healed various diseases and conditions and any of these could have been cancer. The bible doesn't give specific scripture about some diseases or cancer. Diseases on earth and catastrophes are the result of sin upon the earth.

Hence, the scripture from 2 Corinthians 4: 16-18 is vital in understanding.

The most important thing to remember is that we always have hope and eternal life through forgiveness. That's the blessing.

Death

Chapter 3

You hear people say," I'm not going to the funeral because you know I don't do funerals," or "I just don't feel right at funerals," or people saying," I don't feel good about dead bodies". My mother, folks and elders, always used to tell me, "there's nothing to be afraid of around a dead body, he's already gone and can't hurt you. It's the ones living and walking that are the problem and biggest fear!

I've had many relatives pass away, die, move on, or whatever you desire to call it; but one thing is for sure as we're born we're going to die. That's bible, that's word, and bible verse about death. I've been to many funerals for kin, for friends, for teachers, I worked with city leaders, and seen many funerals for TV stars, athletes, dignitaries and I've been a pallbearer at about 4 funerals.

But the topic of death is really critical in the scheme of life, because some have lost a loved one and are not able to move past it. The memories, the love of that person whether it be a mother, friend, child, co-worker or even a pet. Life has a cycle, life has a pattern and some of us get caught up thinking that things will always be the same now and forever.

Things won't be the same, but I guess the loss is harder to shake when it's your spouse, child, mother or father and that definite tools are needed to recover and live the abundant life God desires us to live. But what happens when someone you love dies, and you refuse to move on with life, or you just can't seem to cope and recover?

Death

So death is a topic that few want to talk about, many hide from, some don't understand, but it's sure and inevitable.

Benjamin Franklin coined a quote about death in his 1789 letter regarding the constitution.

In this world nothing can be said to be certain except death and taxes.

Other quotes which relate to death are:

Death is not the opposite of life/ but a part of it....

Life hurts a lot more than death....

Intellectual growth should commence at birth and cease only at death   **Albert Einstein**

Since the day of my birth, my death began its walk. It is walking toward me without hurrying.

Jean Cocteau

Death is the wish of some, the relief of many, and the end of all…

It's strange that they fear death. Life hurts a lot more than death. At the point of death, the pain is over. Jim Morrison

We all have parents, cousins, friends, grandparents, neighbors and church members and others who've crossed on into death and left sadness, broken pieces, and others wondering why.

The saddest moment of my life was in 1992, when my mother died at the age of 51, I was just about to start doing things with her. She was entering the age when she could enjoy the benefits of life and spend time with her grandkids and kids.

God always knows better and has better timing than we do. Even at Longview High school, I crossed a point of when I really was tired of so many of my fellow teachers, students and friends passing away, and I'm left going to another sad funeral. Showing compassion for grieving families, bringing that food over for the week, and the flowers and cards. It shouldn't be a routine, but seemingly it was for me.

So the questions come to mind. Why? How come? What happened? Couldn't God have spared him or her? When is the funeral? More questions than can reasonably be answered.

You just sit back and let God answer those questions. Death is reality and death is inevitable.

So one of the toughest things to get past is the death of a child, parent or friend. What do you do or say when someone has lost a loved one? Do you ask the stupid questions and offer conversations as how did she die? My momma died of that, I think? Has she been sick lately? How did they find her? Did he have Aids? Who killed him and why?

Stay clear of the mental stuff and be quiet or contribute to freeing them up in a positive way. Here's some help:

Understand that no way can you truly know how that person feels at this time. The valuable thing to do is to be present, supportive and not rush to talk or ask

questions. Let the person express themselves and feel their way through their maze of emotions. If you're there at the time, it could be an ear, a consoling hug, a request of drink or food, an

errand, or other. Being present refers to being available, open, being there, or lending an ear.

- 1. Listen and listen, look for openings to talk in short positive tones.

- Stay away from the negative terms of: at least she's in a better place...

- You can always......

- My cousin had that same thing....

- Oh Lord, I know she was in pain with that!

These phrases tend to minimize the extent of the loss and perform opposite effects of love.

A. Be available for help
B. Say the person's name and rewind memories..

C. Deflect those who have no knowledge of comforting others or goal is to exacerbate the moment.

What does the Bible say about death?

1. There's spiritual death and physical death (Genesis 3:22-24)

Physical death is when our bodies cease to function and spiritual death is when we're cut off from everlasting life with God.

2. Everyone is dead without Jesus   Romans 5

3. After death comes judgment

1 Corinthians 15: 35-55

4. Physical death comes to all, but just a door to eternity for the believers

Abundant life is s a big thing.

50

37 Points of Impact
Chapter 4

Monetary
1. Provide incentives for getting to help
2. Avoid placing blame, be positive, be genuine
3. Don't be negative"esp. behind their back
4. Donate Time to them, collect a donation
5. Skills drill, teach them something, give them a job
6. Give them a hotel night

Social
7. *Include them in a group outing*
8. *Offer them a ride to a treatment center*
9. *Support team of friends or trustworthy*

10. *A cookout, Invite them to a meal together*

11. *Acknowledge the situation*
12. *Introduce them to a friend, Facebook friend them*
13. *Ask how they feel ,don't assume*
14. *Express your concern, offer your support*
15. *Take them to a gym, walk together*
16. *Attend a festival together, movie or outing*

17. *Love them and show it genuinely*

Spiritual

18. *Pray, let them pray, ask others to pray for them*
19. *Meeting with a minister/counselor*
20. *Write a letter of formal encouragement*
21. *Avoid placing blame, be positive, be genuine*
22. *Don't be negative, esp. behind their back*

Physical

23. *Offer to help with house work or outside*
24. *Hug him or her*
25. *Give them a hotel night*
26.

Communication

27. *Offer to help take phone calls*
28. *Coordinate a call or card chain*
29. *Get them to the 1st step, refer someone*

Transportation

30. *Get them to needed treatment*
31. *Treatment center, offer a ride*
32. *Offer help with errands, ride them around*

Simple

33. *Let them talk/listen. Don't try to give advice*
34. *Contact an agency for them*
35. *Suggest a doctor, counseling*
36. *Encourage a healthy diet*
37. *Be a compassionate listener, rather than give advice*
38. *Learn about their condition or situation*

Depression
Chapter 5

I talk to people and I've been on the earth long enough to just about see through people. When I was in school I always heard my mother and Grandparents say, if you see somebody always happy and smiling they're either extremely happy, crazy, or wearing a mask of camouflage.

In life these days many of the same stresses and strain still exist but with the advent of financial peer pressure, competition, drugs, the workforce changing, and worry and doubt; many are drifting into states of depression and confusion. I believe parents are also a cause of depression as well as death, PTSD, sexual or physical assaults and medical problems. You probably ask if I have ever been depressed and I will say yes, but I didn't stay in that state.

I've always trusted in God first to strengthen my resolve though prayers, scriptures and going to an encouraging person to relieve my stress. In America today young and

old are taking drugs of all types to get away from stress and depression that make life difficult for them to cope.

Depression chokes off a person's possibilities in life and renders them in doubt and fear. It harnesses one to a chain

of turmoil which prevent one from ever reaching abundant life living. It would definitely be a valuable skill to have the talent and or ability to speak life into someone and release them from depression and ills of negativity.

Do you ever see people happy on payday and Friday, but frustrated and mad on Monday? Many in 2016- and 2017 are stuck into a corner where they wear masks of happiness to present to people daily and camouflaging aloof of hurt. Facebook is another tool where the average person can identify another with depression or a depressed life. No one is that happy about life where you always post things speaking about yourself and speaking of yourself.

One man's quote said that, the loudest person in the room is the weakness person in the room. I believe that and can witness that in cyber land too. One thing is that

few have learned to deal with their problems, but not realizing that God sendeth sunshine on the just and unjust.

Depression can lead to hurting ourselves, apathy, or even suicide.

How wonderful it would be to be able to deliver someone from depression and apathy?

How can you help someone with depression in real life? I ask this, because people are being held in bondage by this demon.

First we must understand that depression is a chronic physical illness with symptoms that are mostly invisible.

Everyone's depression is different from sadness to short term jubilance and a mountainside back to a rainbow of emotions, wrapped in frustration.

It will cause your friends and relatives to withdraw from you and destroy your ability to produce at work and lead to death.

That makes it crucial and important.

Studies believes on the outside that only 38 % of people believe that depression is a real health problem.

1. Don't shame people for being negative, if the pattern persists as a daily occurrence, know that they might be connected positive to negative response.
2. Refuse to say you're something else or you're too much. This statement can send the individual down the cliff of despair.
3. Encourage them to follow needed medication to level their spirits out, don't dispute their so-called needs; suggest doctor evaluation.
4. Understand that the depressed person's ability to find the positive in their life is almost impossible, because it doesn't usually exist in their framework.

5. Limit your interactions and focus in on small things and build on that, as," I like your hair and your new this or that ".
6. Know that depression doesn't mean sadness, but it does mean fatigue, disordered thinking, and sleep issues.

7. Reality thinking is not the answer and understand they do see the elephant in the room.

Biblically Speaking

What does the Bible say about depression?

As Christians we aren't guaranteed a beautiful rainbow life without trials and mountains, but we are promised hope, peace and a savior for our sins.

We have joy, hope and freedom from life's issues or to deal with life's issues.

So act on the truth, the causes and circles around love.

DIVORCE

Chapter 6

People say, never say never and marriage never was meant to be a temporary or conditional thing. We go into it with strong vows made before God and pledging to commit to our soulmate till death do us part.

Marriage seems to have slowed up, divorce rates have risen and I look around and see people getting married for the 1st time at age 30 and 40. Some choose not to get married, but shack up or live together or even just enter into numerous casual relationships without strong commitment.

What happened to these days where a man met a woman and fell in love at the age of 23-25 and had that big wedding with all the fancy colors and food and hundreds of people and maids of honors and grooms?

Those days are past it seems, although people in their 60's still get married from time to time; and this compliments both parties like a business proposition for old age. I guess values have changed, some people have no fear of God, and some just grow into selfishness or a state of independence where it's hard to support, rely, and follow the guidelines of another.

I don't know about the answers, but I do know divorce can cause a hardship for women, men and kids. Divorce will prevent a person from releasing that shackle and securing the abundant life Christ desires us to have.

It's October, and we're on the edge of 2017, but in many ways of matrimony we've fallen behind. This is a critical mountain slide which hinders youth development educationally, socially, and especially spiritually. Parent's often bad mouth the other parent and this creates dysfunctional families and it's felt in the church, the school and in the community.

What do you do if the remnants of that divorce is hampering your emotional state or that of your kids? There has to be some way to get past this and not be

mired in the mud of negativity. There has to be!!!

So how can you talk to or help a divorced person when their consistent conversation is negative about their ex and their past marriage?

I mean help them get past this pain...

- Respect their privacy and don't agree or disagree and take sides.

- Don't judge or ridicule them, it may come back on you.

* Socialize with them as you can. Invite them to events and still be their friend.

- Help them get back to a normal, regular style of life.

- Don't push them to date, it takes different people on their own time.

- Let them talk and just listen, but don't get bombarded with negativity.

- Don't place blame or talk behind their backs.

- Provide ongoing support and understand it's not about you.

What the Bible says about divorce

Many see divorce as a possible solution to a troubled and damaged marriage. It's a breakdown of small community and

exchanges the pain, horror, stress and emotions for another couple.

Marriage is an agreement, a covenant, and a partnership.

Malachi 2:16

God instituted marriage for a purpose. When questioned about marriage by the Pharisees, Jesus points them to God's purpose for marriage.) Matthew 19:3-9)

One purpose…mirror God's image

2nd purpose….completion of each other and companionship

3rd purpose….multiply and create a God legacy

Divorce has exceptions as death and adultery (Matthew 19:8)

Seek God's guidance before a divorce and during a marriage and allow him to order your steps.

Sometimes people today are blinded by the media's portrayal of love and happiness.

Emotional or Mental Problems
Chapter 7

It's a complicated issue and one very few know much about or care to even deal with for some fear or unknown reason. You see the men walking the long miles from the Hwy 80 rescue mission to the east side of Longview's shady motels at the intersection of Hwy 80 and Eastman road. You see women and you see men, but you rarely see kids and this is a daily stroll in search of some unknown food, water, friends, money, drugs, or something else?

You see the man, Tim standing in front of Walmart or rainy days, cold days, and near him is his pile of junk and leftover burger paper and the waves and talks to himself and people

stop and feed him; feeling sorry for him. You see the woman pulling the big wagon loaded with all her belongings and she

parks at Whataburger and she parks at Eastman and Hwy and she seems sad talking to herself, but what and how can you help them? You see the elderly woman walking down high street to the mall and turning around and walking to the

Treehouse apartments and down to Estes parkway and making her trip throughout the day no matter what the weather is. We all have family members who exhibit strange behaviors that endanger our family or affecting their life and their kids. You hear the stories, you read the papers and you see the news headlines. Many of these situations involves the hidden people in our society: those with emotional and mental problems.

You see the man shrouded in clothes off his body and walking as a slave and looking in terror and he pulls a box or is draped in a sheet or blanket on a hot or cold day.

I don't know what they search for or where they're coming from or even where they live, but one thing you must know is that the streets have a life of their own when night falls. You see them on the corner standing and some wait to cross the street and some take the initiative to cross and jaywalk and disregard any traffic laws or rules. Many will be standing and waiting the cross and seemingly to be in a conversation with themselves, or some will

interact with drivers and motion for money or some profane gestures at you. It's sometimes disturbing and you want to lock your doors, and you get a line of fear in your soul and you see the raw side of life up close and personal. Nobody I know ever talks about this subject, but I do bring it up and people let me know in

strange fashion that they see this going on, but never concerned themselves

with it. Some of these individuals have been arrested, some are felons, some prostitutes, some have emotional baggage, some mental baggage, some are drug addicts, and some are just regular folks tossed out of society because they have shown their families or the community that they had problems. I'm bringing this up, I'm concerned, I care and I want to make a difference because it's my mission as a Christian to care, the bible and Jesus have commanded me to

care. The sad reality is that some of these individuals fear help, don't want help and some are dangerous, because they see you as a threat and all the want is money or drugs. So how do you help them? So how do you affect their lives and intervene in their world safely and beneficially?

You're also the the minister pushing Christ and bolding standing on the corner with his tie and sign preaching loudly to the traffic drivers.

Why are we so silent?

What is the answer or what do we do?

I can't be the only one who cares!

God loves them and us all, right?

Why does it seem like a segment of our society maybe 70 % only concern is how they look or the money make in their life?

Studies say 25 % of the American population has some sort of mental issues and diagnosing it is a very complex issue.

Schizophrenia

Bipolar

1. Diagnosing the illness correctly
2. Encourage the loved one and for them to get help
3. Don't be judgmental, be reassuring
4. **Studies various mental illnesses**
5. **Talk to a professional and a minister**

6. Decide between the possible: their needs and lifestyle

7. Get a group or small group of supportive family to work together for good.

Anxiety   dementia psychotic behaviors

Mood disorders   eating disorders

Depression

We are a fallen generation and sin has created destruction in our very communities and families. All of us suffer from some sort of mental

something. Sin can lead to sickness, because it separates us from God and creates an atmosphere for the devils works to build.

We in this me me me generation suffer a mental situation and we want

to run to the psychiatrist, but we must establish a mode or standard where we go to God to deal with the sins first, then let him direct us to earthly hell as needed.

Mark 7: 21-23

Proverbs 3: 3-8

Chapter 8

I've never been in a situation of being unemployed and looking for income to support myself and /or my family.

America in the last 12 years has undergone changes affecting the job market, housing market and this is attributed to oil, gas, banks , mortgages , greed among executives and this has trickled down to regulate people like you and I . You can't blame one area for this problem. In the Bush years we fell behind and President Obama brought some relief. Unemployment compensation and part times jobs became the thing.

It has to be a bad feeling to need a job to provide income and your family, spouse, or friends pressure you and put you in a shell of negativity making you feel less than a man.

When the oil price dropped and America stopped drilling abundantly many young men lost their jobs and it made it so

bad because many lived a high class like of 5,000 or so a month and were able to travel, buy cars, and anything they

wanted or needed. It was a glorious time and there's no better feeling than being able to support yourself.

Now, out of work, the real pressures of family pop up which breeds divorce, confusion, desire to do whatever to get that income gain or even suicide in rare cases.

It's sometimes a silent killer but how to you go back to $ 10 an hour when you're accustomed to a lot more.

What are the answers? What and how do you cope and put food on your table? Bills and needs don't stop.

They don't stop.

No need for me to be spreading news of gloom and pessimism that there are no jobs out there or that there are plenty jobs out there and you're just not looking hard enough.

Some studies show there is no direction connection between unemployment and marital dissatisfaction.

How can you help someone going through a period of unemployment, and despair?

1. They need to talk about it and put it out there into a reality.
2.
3. Don't blame or judge the individual
4. Reach out to them and take them to dinner, Starbucks, church or something to change the mood and spirit.
5. Don't nag , encourage
6. Reward and encourage every step forward or attempt.
7. Put things in perspective and brain storm with great strategies

What does the bible say about employment and working?

Americans spend about 50% of their waking hours working.

The beginning of work started in Genesis 1:1-

Where the bible says that God worked for 6 days and rested on the 7th. These passages revealed the essence of work in God's eyes. God is innately good, so work in basically good.

God created man in his own image and created him to cultivate the garden.

Because of the fall of man, God instituted a new relationship with man and work. God transformed man from eating from the garden to the field where he would labor through his life, through sorrow and toil.

Genesis 3:17

1 Timothy 5:8

Worse than an infidel

The Forgotten, Invisible American / the Homeless

Chapter 9

You've seen them in your town, your city, your neighborhood and in parks and at the bus transit station. The homeless? They're in groups, they're on corners of busy intersections and at times they're on your street, walking past you.

Oh, if you look around in Houston or some of the major cities they'll be gathered up under freeways and over passes begging, sleeping, pan handling or being a nuisance by begging and loitering in public places.

You can't miss them and you can't avoid, but what's the answer?

What do you do to help a person in this situation? They put themselves in your path to interact with you and possibly get a hand out or trick you.

How do you help them? Give them money or not? Give them religion? Pray for them? Ignore them? Arrest them? So what are the stats for homelessness? In America about 500,000 people are homeless on any given night, 200,000 were people in families, 350,000 were individuals, 15 % or 80,000 are considered chronically homeless and 2% or 13,000 are considered homeless in families, 8 % or 50,000 are homeless veterans.

Studies from the blank show that the main reason people are homeless is because they cannot find affordable housing in their urban area, scarcity of affordable housing, and inability to maintain housing. The numbers and information comes from Point in time

counts which is operated by a requirement from the Department of Housing and Urban Development (HUD).

Most Families typically become homeless, because of an unforeseen financial crisis as a medical emergency, car accident, and death in the family that keeps them from maintaining housing.

Youth become homeless due to family conflict, abuse, neglect, or family divorce; many times this is short term and they return after a short stint on the streets. Veterans become homeless because of was related disabilities, mental anguish, PTSD, and difficulty dealing with

civilian life. These problems can lead to alcoholism, drug addiction, and violent behavior in the community.

Chronic homelessness is the public face of homelessness; it involves long term homelessness. People in this category usually live in shelters and consume the majority of homeless assistance as a result.

How can you help a homeless person?

1. Pray…This includes gaining some repoire with them and getting the church involved and/or when possible.
2. Donate money to reputable agencies. Or to the person directly, if safe. Items .such as

3. items to help them keep warm or cool: shoes, hats, coats, socks and hygiene items.
4. Donating new or used items to sound organizations: or to the person directly, if safe. Items .such as items to help them keep warm or cool: shoes, hats, coats, socks and hygiene items.
5. Create jobs for them if you're able to offer them work that can support their needs.
6. Donate food to shelters and churches which feed the homeless.
7. Contact needed help for them and get them on the path to recovery.
8. Call emergency services, especially if they appear in danger to others or themselves.

9. Remember if a person is locked in homelessness they are often prevented from living life and adequately moving toward their goals and often this can develop into a state of despair. Sometimes listening can be the answer in patience.

Chapter 10

You hear about it, but it's never on your street, in your family, among your group or friends. Suicide is real. It seems like God is placing this topic in the forefront of my book to reach out to the hurting. It also seems that all the 7 topics I discussed through the book earlier can be a factor contributing to suicide. It's not just the teenager whose boyfriend broke up with her, the couple going through a nasty divorce and one of them wants to end their lives, the individual with mental problems or the elderly person tired of suffering. Its real life and on your street, in your family, in your church and daily happening. Why?

Depression is the common problem in many suicides and it can be diagnosed or undiagnosed. There is truly no one thing that can indicate suicide. There are things that increase likelihood of suicide as anxiety, substance abuse and depression.

When stress factors exceed the ability of the individual to cope with daily factors, then suicide is a very present threat.

Changes in behavior or new behavior previously unidentified need to be monitored. Changes from a painful loss or event can often trigger behavior changes.

There are many factors to look for from their talk, their moods, isolation, depression, and substance abuse.

Risk factors increasing chances are related mental and emotional problems, stressful events as bullying, family or friend death and job related; also previous history of suicide in the family.

How do you prevent suicide?

1. Understand suicide is a cry for help and few realize the impact of it.
2. Take them seriously and it's better to give help sooner than later. Include someone in their life to change their thoughts or moods. Be honest and genuine.

3. Talk to them about it and ask the question, but be willing to provide a source for professional help.
4. Know that most people think about suicide, **but only 2%** really go through with it.
5. Listen and avoid giving advice and arguing and they'll know you care.

84

Da Millennials/ Generation Y
Chapter 11

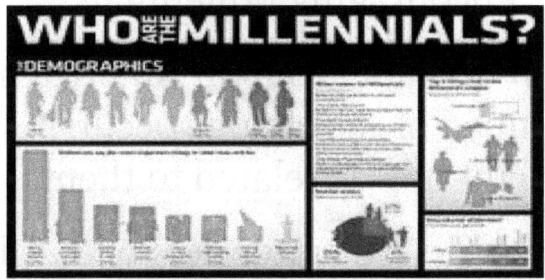

Here I am sitting in the Alpine Church of Christ service listening, not to our regular minister, but to a youth minster named Logan.

He's preaching a sermon talking about relationships and goals with Jesus. Now he's

talking about reaching out to a critical group of the American population, millennials.

This is so amazing to me, because basically all 3 of my kids are in this millennial age zone.

I'm going to sleep with this on my mind and God is directing me to placing a section of my book toward reaching and encouraging Millennials.

They're the hot group in America now and much of the change occurring in right now is related to them.

So I guess we better deal with this subject and expose you to characteristics of this age bracket and how we can communicate and reach them.

Millennials are known as the Generation Y, and the Generation Me. Brother Logan referred to them as between the ages of **22-35,**

but different agencies vary that age group from 1996-1997 birth years.

We'll use the ages of **22-40** for simplicity.

- Many of the millennials are digital minded and generally enjoy living and working in the urban area.
- * Many in the (Generation Me) shower greater traits of narcissism and entitlement

It researched that Millennials will have more buying power than any other age group by the year 2017, but their spending differs greatly from their parents.

- Few millennials can afford to own a home and many live with parents
- They usually don't buy in bulk, because they're single or their families are small.
- Millennials are marrying at a **26 % rate.** Choosing to live together or other lifestyles.

When they talk about marriage, many millennials say, they'll wait until they're financially stable.

Many don't know about manual cars or cars made before 2000.

Baby boomers prefer the traditional beers while millennials prefer Indie brand and new stuff.

Very few millennials invest in stocks, bonds, and savings for future.

Many Millennials spend a great share of their income of phones, tablets, pc and some even refrain from having to.

How to we reach the Millennials?

1. *Expect to use social media to reach them*

2. *Millennials think dimly of church and religion and we must be real and relevant to reach them*

3. *They expect clarity and genuineness and sincerity living*

4. *They want positive mentors and peers who will speak their language*

5. *Person to person interaction and understand variety is the mode to reach them.*

Inspirational Poetry Corner

Chapter 12

I See Masks

I see masks....
I see fences...
Built to keep intruders and strangers from entering zones of emotion.

And I see people hurting, looking for eternal Band-Aids to ease them from the hurt of yesterday.

But they don't understand that Band-Aids are temporary... and their purpose is for one day.

I see masks...
I used to wear one....
Never again....

Hurt people...

Hiding their hurt

Hiding their fear

The Waiting Room

Born into sin, been trampled by temptations, lost in this world and burdened by hate.

The world say….what's gonna happen is gonna happen

I trust God not led by fate

And what the world puts on you can often be too much

See the world's watching and wondering

And wondering what they see

But we gotta grow and we gotta know

That

The Christ in me might be the only Christ they see

And the world will grab you by your neck and squeeze and squeeze until you choak.

And this can be your friends, strangers or even kinfolk.

So I'm in the waiting room

But I didn't check in myself

God set up the appointment

To tighten up my spiritual health

Time for me to get closer to him,

Cause his fullness is worth worth than wealth

He's turning me golden to get more of his anointment

And that's why I sit in this waiting room

Waiting on his holy appointment

But in this waiting room ain't no time to worry and ain't no time to fret

I got a place for you to be

And my son, you gonna be there

But you ain't there yet.

As the world changes and some but not all my children are falling

You live for me

Cause people in the street are hurting and calling

Searching for a Christ who can heal their soul

Cause living for the devil and the world gets old

So if you find yourself in the waiting room, waiting for him to show you the path

Waiting for that man for you, job for you

Or any direction that you're hoping God will lead

You just keep living for him
And daily keep planting seeds and stay
In the waiting room
Until he calls for you to come out of the
Waiting room.

Abundant Life

See I was a lump of coal way down in the earth

That was my start that was my birth

And by description I was worthless

No value, no worth

Without direction, without purpose

But God shook things up with heat and with fire

Changing this sinner from corruption

Changing my heart

The devil is a liar

And now I'm on a new road

New destination

New purpose

New plan

Headed to a place not made by hands

I stand for right cause he showed his light

Cleaned my soul

Now imam diamond worth more than gold

Not meek, I'm, standing on his word

To fight all fears

I know the darts of the devil, has more than one

He has several

I revel in love

Eyes wide open knowing the thief cometh but to steal, and to kill and destroy

Won't put me on a string like a puppet or a toy

But I serve a winning team, no longer hurt by sin's sting

Trampled by bitterness and strife

I serve a king who died to bring us and me eternal, abundant life..

But I didn't check in myself

God set up the appointment

To tighten up my spiritual health

Time for me to get closer to him,

Cause his fullness is worth more than wealth

He's turning me golden get more of his anointment

And that's why I sit in this **waiting room**

On this holy appointment

But in this waiting room ain't no time to worry or and ain't no time to fret

I got a place for you to be and

My son, you gonna be there

But you ain't there yet

As the world changes and some but not all my children are falling

You live for me

Cause people in the street are hurting and calling

Searching for a Christ who can heal their soul

Cause living for the devil and the world gets old

So if you find yourself in th**e waiting room,** waiting for him to show you the path

Waiting for that man for you, job for you

Or any direction that you hoping God will lead

You just keep living for him

And daily keep planting seeds

And stay

In the waiting room

Until he calls for you to come out of

The waiting room

In Da 17

Hm... I smile but real is just real in every situation, whether its reality or not for you.

*

And I ain't in the arena or business of entertaining you cause, hey that's the problem we've been getting and being entertained too long...

.that's not what's gonna change us. Time to be enlightened and educated

Time for sincerity and truth and for hearts to mend.

I come to remind me first and you that too many of us are living life and don't know we're living for...whether it's because you got the wrong person in your ear or you're not connected

with a source from above that can transform you and release into all the potentials and abilities that you truly possess..

See voices are changing and its time in Da 17 to start living for something..

Too many of us are trapped in the book of Malachi and the although the key is near we'll never seem to find it.

Living in a purgatory that transcends through generations and locks us in a circle of nothingness.

*

I ain't called to be popular, but I am called to set the captives free, how can I do that if I ain't free.

Too many of us are sending people where we won't go and where they don't want to go...looking for love in all the wrong places and our communities and us can't heal unless we acknowledge the sickness....and medicine in a white pill bottle ain't always the answer...

We need to have faith in him and ourselves even when we don't see the staircase..

Too many of us are still in an unstable stage of puberty, locked into stagnant dementia and thinking that we're really on

top of the world cause we got a pretty house car or 1,000 in the bank...but

blind in a sea of purgastory and purgatory.

And I don't mean to offend. I'm here on grace and truth from God and taught by my elders, mother, teachers and real friends on which I have a minimal amount.

But in that I know your call never matches your background and to change people I gotta scare people enough to make them look into the mirror of hope and empower men to think and know that coke and water address the same thirst but water is better for you.

*

We have power, but I don't need a title

I'm not a politician, I'm just an advocate for good

But maybe America ain't ready or used to a confident black man who cares for real

Shed some light and create an environment for learning and in conjunction with sharing.

We gotta stop following leaders who lived too long with the wrong message. Filling their pockets and our unfulfilled hopes

Church gotta stop keeping truth in the house and learn religion can't save nobody and churches shouldn't have walls while you're telling me what I should do and you ain't doing it..

And black lives do matter, if somebody in blue kills them as victims but not if a Black man from our hood kills them?

candlelight vigils and marches don't address the problem in a band-aidal mentality.

*

When we're constantly talking about have a happy new years and reason for the season and constantly being trained

to observe every holiday and release or power of our dollar to capitalism and another Mexican grocery, restaurant, or popular brand or chain that brainwashed our soul and we're stagnant on beauty shops and detail shops....making 100's while they make millions, and we smiling saying I saved some money and I'm the only one with this pair.

And sometimes you gotta burn bridges to grow like Christ wants you to

Smiling in my face and bringing your bull ..to my doorstep.

*

I smell a rat playing word chess and I feel sorrow for Charleston, Ferguson and Dallas but I feel sorrow for my Longview eastside too.

we're living in an age where in some people's minds animals are worth more than men

an arrogance floating in the air as thick as pollution and choking men with feeble minds and not realizing that some arrogant never went from the top and seen the residue and the bottom of life.

Arrogance with a memory of hate is dangerous.

Many at the top never got a roundtrip ticket from the bottom.

*

Vodka and Hennessey never saved a soul and writing checks for a cause don't connect on a personal level like quality time and a parade, turkey leg or community festival aint gon pierce twisted hearts.

There is still hope

But we gotta stay clear of hypocrisy of trusting and thinking a man bankrupt 4 times and married 3 can lead us into a promise land..

We must love ourselves...we gotta love ourselves...to affect change..

Maybe America ain't ready for a confident, empowered black man..It should be and needs to get ready...

And at times we're the best at forgiving as a community, if we get a confession,

Know that the carpenter never created nothing but transformed hearts....

And compassion gotta combine with conviction and false humility and lack of knowledge are spiraling us into the twilight zone.

Its time..

*

But we can't lead where we won't go

It's time to educate ourselves on truth...and hope

And plant seeds of hope

I and he that watered are equal, God gives the increase

We gotta Free people

But free yourself first

Now run tell dat

Faded White Picket Fences

I still have dreams of white picket fences

New car in the driveway, wife named Ruby and 3 kids running around the yard like today was their last day to play.

But what's love got to do with it, cause if I remember correctly, love ain't never paid my bills.

Dreams of having a job that allowed me to be and do what I wanted, not worrying bout borrowing money from my brother, mother, cousin, or friend.

Having a big color TV in the living room filled with every station that they offer: Cinemax, and Showtime and any other one that I want.

New car in the driveway, wife named Ruby and 3 kids running around the yard like today was their last day to play.

But what's love got to do with it, cause if I remember correctly, love ain't never paid my bills.

And 2 cars will never be enough for me even though my garage only fit 2, in this capitalistic generation, you need a few

In a position where I could have 3 credit cards, and when I come to the restaurant or store they know me so well, I don't need to show an ID or sign my name.

New car in the driveway, wife named Ruby and 3 kids running around the yard like today was their last day to play.

What's love got to do with it, cause if I remember correctly, love ain't never paid my bills.

And I still have dreams of a friendly mailman who knows me and where to put my mail, even when I'm not there.

And I still think that I want a dog names Spot and cat named Buttons, but as I write this I think my dreams are fading, because to don't paint the picture of real life.

New car in the driveway, wife named Ruby and 3 kids running around the yard like today wad their last day to play.

But what's love got to do with it, cause if I remember correctly, love ain't never paid my bills.

And now

My faded white picket fence just fell down.

Snakes Don't Hiss No More....

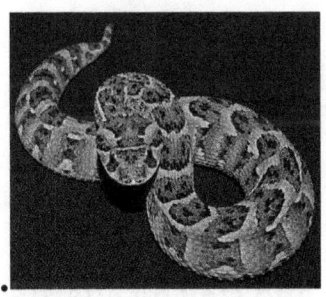

Snakes don't hiss no more

They call you baby, brother or friend

get close enough to know your weaknesses and strengths

and when you let your guard down they bite and do you end..

Snakes don't hiss no more

cause they know that's the sound and behavior that people expect

always want a favor or loan

hard to say no, but you don't they'll keep you in debt

Snakes don't hiss no more but they still

curl up, slide and hide
examples of cowards
locked up in their pride
so keep your shoes on when you out
strolling through the yard

and keep alert
and stay on guard
cause snakes don't hiss no more
they call you baby, brother or friend
and with a knife in one hand and
evil intentions..and an evil grin
their goal is to do you end...

cause
Snakes don't hiss no more

You Can't Hear Cause You Got That Roach in Your Ear

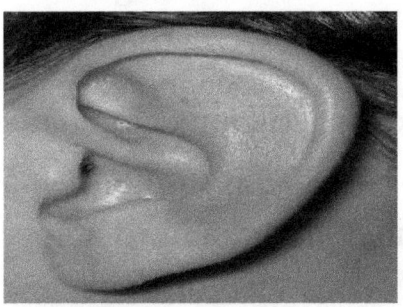

I look around and not because I want to, but hey it seems to turn like that....be like that....flow like that and it ain't like....I don't control or can't control the situation. PS...I don't try to control people and you can't control me.

It's the fact that imma let a lil happen to show you..Teach you...cause the best

teaching come when you bust your own self in the head. ?

And before I can benefit you, I got to have my stuff on track, together, lined up, squared up, in tune with and for me. Cause the blind can't lead the blind unless both fall in the ditch.

Just think, 2012, you was at that point, this point, this position, and now on the edge of 2017 and you ain't moved from that.

Spiritually beaten, financially broke

Physically out of shape emotionally unstable

Kids lacking

(and you still ain't got no man)

Or either sharing one, or limited to a baby daddy who don't even buy pampers once a month.

Following Ronnie, Bobby, Ricky, Mike and Schneka to a confusion they also share.

Flooding your mind, telling you to run this way and that...saying gurl I wouldn't take that ..or do that

Following a mess, scheme this way..saying gurl, I wouldn't take that

And none of them seems to put you in the spot

Whew you can be you

Do you   live for you?

And be the man or woman who

Can satisfy his needs
Makes me wonder
Where you'll be in 2022
Now look in the mirror and fix your face
And your life
I'm just saying

Thinking Outside the Box

Stuck in your zone, been in this warp for quite a long time..

Always broke, in dispute, or in a money bind

Running on fumes, not led by a goal

Same today as yours was years ago

Like moistured bathroom mold

Say you gonna do this and promise you'll do that

Why is it 10 years later?

You stuck where you're at

You see life one way and through one fine straight tunnel

Like when we was kids looking through that paper towel funnel

You really think life gonna put aspiration and achievement flat dab in your hand ?

Can't see what's on the water if you keep standing and looking on land

Never can work with others, always stuck in your own point of view

You know there's other colors in the coloring box, but all you see is blue.....

See there's a world bigger than you waiting for you to inspect

Stretch your horizons loosen up your neck...

Stop hating on life, daily kicking your rocks...

You can't see God's blessing for you

Unless you learn to think outside the box.

Motivational Short Stories

Chapter 13

Poolside Chat

While working at the recreation center and decided to stroll and check on things. I went to the pool area and saw the lifeguard, Robert talking with a swimmer. I asked them both what would you say to someone in 37 seconds if they were facing extreme difficulties in their life . The swimmer answered, " I'd pray for them and Robert said, " I'd tell them I love them". I smiled and those them that I never thought of those answers. It came to me that sometimes you just rub their shoulder or grab their hand, say I love and I'm praying for you ! That's enough !

God Is Using You For Good

It was 6pm, and we were meeting in the Longview Library for play practice on a Thursday. I told the cast members to gather at the back of the library near the far corner; that would allow us to read over our parts. About 15 members were gathering, but the far corner, hideaway spot was occupied by a woman studying.

For about 5 minutes we looked puzzled, because the middle section wasn't large enough room to gather and have some privacy. So this lone person in the corner was really thwarting our plans to hide in the corner.

We chatted about what to do, and I decided to see if the lady would move to the middle. I

kindly asked her, "Hi, we're trying to meet for a motivation play reading and wanted to know if you would move, so we could have this large table and chairs?"

She looked up in surprise and said, "sure, no problem, I can easily slide over there, I'm almost ready to go anyway!"

The group assembled in her spot as she moved and as I stood on the side and looked, she walked up to me.

I need to tell you something. God told me he's using you to change people and things. He sees a lot in you and he's gonna use you to bless others.

I stood speechless and simply said, "thank you."

Then I turned my head and, it was like she vanished. I go to the library often and never remember seeing her.

Life is Short

It was the 1st weekend of February and I went home to Houston to celebrate the Super Bowl weekend. I was searching Facebook on the Friday before leaving and scanned a few of my classmates' Facebook pages. I noticed 3 classmates in a picture and they had made a comment about one of my favorites in the photo. I didn't know who they were referring to and why, so I scrolled down in alarm. I went to another friend's page and put things together. It was Doug, one of the most extroverted, happiest people I've ever met. He even come from Houston to my book signing 2 years ago and was one of my leading supporters to congratulate me on my completing my first motivational book. He stayed through my book signing, bought an autographed copy, shook my hand, hugged me; and told me he was proud of me.

This was something outstanding, but customary for someone of his class. It gave me new life and fulfilled the connection I needed to motivate even more people. Doug, the one who was an athlete, the student who was smart and the girls' said was very handsome, the all American guy, who was not for Black or white or sold on a clique or special interest group. He was outspoken for sure, but he was Doug. He loved everyone and didn't feel like the low man or the high man should be neglected or favored. I knew this cause we were classmates since 12 years old. In the past 5 years, I saw on his Facebook post and comments that he didn't hate President Obama like many did. He only wanted people to get a fair chance in life.

So this saddened my weekend and put mystery into why the all-American guy left us so soon. Someone then said that he was hurting too much.

I won't and can't speculate on that, but life can take us through turns that make us wonder what to do. I pray for his soul, his family and those that remember him to honor his spirit of joy and love.

I'll forever remember Doug's smile and energy.

I'll most remember how Doug came from Houston to support me at my book signing in 2014. During the signing, I read a poem called, "I Don't want to be Average", cause average ain't good enough for me. I watched as he listened on the back row and smiled as I recited it. Afterwards he hugged me and said, I'm proud of you Terrell.

He put a picture on his Facebook page with a caption saying, "

I had the privilege to be at the book signing for my friend, Terrell Glen Edwards. His new book is titled, "Vegetable Soup for the Soul". The talk was very inspirational. I am very proud for you and of you my old classmate,

Doug

The little things make all the difference.

I'm 6' 5"

"I Said, I Like Tall Guys, But..."

It was Sunday night, and I was leaving Luby's after buying some soup. I decided that I'd better get some gas and a newspaper to start the week. I hurried into the convenience store, and as I entered I rushed to the restroom and the back of the store to check for newspapers. A lady was at the counter doing a transaction and she stared at me, and I glanced at her.

In 3 minutes I came back to the counter to pay for my gas and the newspaper, and she was still at the counter;

somebody outside was bringing her something. She was at the counter paying with a credit card for her items and the clerk said, "Ma'am, yours will take a few minutes; let the gentleman go first. She backed up and stood beside me, I noticed her staring at me from head to toe.

After a few seconds, she said, "You're tall". "How tall are you "? I said, "Take a guess". She said," Oh about 7 foot"? I said, "No" She guessed again 6'9" and the clerk looked surprised. I held my hand up and she said, "5'6"," I said noooo, 6'5"". She said, "Oh you're tall! I said, "how tall are you, and she said with heels 5'1". I said, "You look taller".

She said, really I'm about 5' 2". I paid for mine as she stared and kindly told the them both, Have a blessed new year". She then

stated that she hoped 2017 was not bad like 2016. I told her , God gonna make it right for you, here's a scripture, Luke 4:18, and I repeated it for them both. She smiled and repeated it for correction, Luke 4:18?

I dropped off this word and hopefully it would germinate. We gotta use every opportunity to reach people, especially every time we encounter them. Free people! Luke 4:18

288 and Almeda/

Houston

It was 5 a.m. and we were heading to Houston for a Jamaica cruise from Galveston. We were now in Houston and I chose to stop and eat breakfast at Alfreda's, a south Houston soul food restaurant. As we exited hwy. 288, we saw a lady walking who was throwing paper in the air as she tore it. We didn't understand, but when you're in the city

you see strange things and this was one of them.

We strolled on down Calais Street to the restaurant, where we saw a man next to it looking around the parking lot. You know you're always attentive when strangers are seemingly have mental issues and situations loitering around a place you desire to enter.

You take notice, you size them and their intentions up. He seemed to be panhandling for those who were parking to enter Alfreda's.

We entered, ordered our breakfast and set and enjoyed it. We saw the woman

who was tearing paper from earlier, as we looked through the window. We just shook our heads and knew alot of homeless people have mental issues and situations that were caused by some hardship or hereditary line in life. Sometimes all you can do is pray.

We finished out meal and exited to the car, as the man we saw earlier came to our vehicle. We guessed he wanted money or to wash our windows for money. We immediately rolled

our windows up and locked our doors in caution. I told my wife, I hope I don't have to use my 9 mm, you never know. Then she said, "He wants money".

I though on it and pulled out some change for him. He pushed a trach in his throat and talked to us in a microphonic tone, asking us where we were from. We rolled the window down, he was a disable vet; he had been a student at the same college where my wife attended and had played college baseball there. 53 years old walking the streets of Houston, panhandling for money or doing odd jobs to make a living, but seemingly in the right state of mental factories.

We had an intriguing conversation about Texas College, Prairie View, and

life in the 80's and the people we knew. It's strange how we can prejudge someone based on appearance and get it

wrong. The lady tearing paper was still on the bust street corner doing her strange behavior. Interacting with people is the only way we're going to see their need and bless them.

Sometimes people go through hardships in life.

It was a good morning on why 288 and Almeda.

We met someone special.

Evolution of a Dream

She was 24, 4 kids, 3 baby daddies living with Momma, no place of her own.

Had dreams of the perfect life, kids, husband, great job and home

Fell in a trap, a hole when she was 15---got told, 'I love you" by a dealer, a dope fiend.

Now there's a little one, soon followed by 3 others, started with a little girl, now she has 3 baby brothers.

Forced to quit school cause Momma had a job and couldn't keep her kids.

Better chance at employment, when they started school and got big.

Restless at night and frustrated in the day – feed the kids, change the diapers, rarely time to sleep or lay we all get stuck in a rut—make those choices, that's the price we have to pay.

She's now 19, and has the world on top of her shoulders, not dreaming any dreams –still getting older. Never goes to church and has completely given up on God.

Imprisoned in strife, life has steadily been hard.

Meets a dude named Matt while shopping at the local Walmart one day....

Asks her out on a date..

She's befuddled about what to say

Shrinks out a, "yes" and that might have changed her life.

Matt is 25, Christian, hardworking and looking for a wife. Not hindered by people's past cause he's changed the one he used to know. Now he's on a God track, his life is full of glow!
But on a Saturday night, 3 months from the time they met.

She's confronted by her exes' gurl and sadly she gets shot. She lays on the parking lot, clinging to life, remembers her kids, and Matt, revisits her life.

Gets rushed to Good Shepherd on the edge of death...doctors tell her family she has one 1 hour left. She opens her eyes by chance, and mumbles" I want to live".

Although this is her desire,

Life is God's to give.....The family huddles to pray and speak life into her situation..

And for 2 hours they sit quietly and pray in patience. In the lobby there's tears and sorrow at the dilemma they're facing.

But in rushes the doctor smiling and joyous...saying, "Family, Megan will see a tomorrow

A life was lost, now years have been borrowed...

1 year later she's married in bliss

Got her GED, and on her way to college...

Off the 'I'm just surviving list!

This story is more common than you could ever imagine.

I'm sure you've heard this story..

It can't be of newness to you

Hold your criticism and judgmental evils

Focus on planting seeds and speaking life into people.

Cause this is the evolution of a

        Evolution of a Dream

Free People

It was July/2016 and I had accepted the offer to be in a comedy event, which was a remake a "In Living Color. My assignment was to play the bad attitude clown called" Homie the Clown"

It would be a fun role in a show to change the mood in Longview, Texas; which was experiencing various unsolved murders in the community. I went to the Christian thrift store to find some shoes and try to formulate a clown

costume resembling Homie's. I found some large shoes that I could paint and as I was at the counter to purchase them, I saw a very bizarre display of t-shirts.

They were kind of a blue jeans scattered blue and the said the words, "free people, side by side twice. Under the big words was a scripture in small print, Luke 4:18. I couldn't stop wondering what the shirt, "free people implied. I asked the clerk and she said it meant to get people out of the bondage of the pressures of the world and sin.

God wants people free and living the abundant life. I nodded as I understood and told her I'd be back to buy 2 ; one for me and one for my wife. I find few shirts with powerful encouraging meanings.

I had hoped to return the next day, Friday to buy the shirts and forgot. I returned to the store about 1 month later and purchased 2 shirts to wear proudly and live by.

I knew at the point I first saw the shirts that God was wanting me to help in freeing people from their fears, burdens, weights, ignorances and their negativity.

Luke 4:18 New Life Version (NLV)
[18] "The Spirit of the Lord is on me. He has put His hand on me to preach the Good News to poor people. He has sent me to heal those with a sad heart. He has sent me to tell those who are being held that they can go free. He has sent me to make the blind to see and to free those who are held because of trouble.

Free People

2nd Chances

By
Terrell Glen Edwards

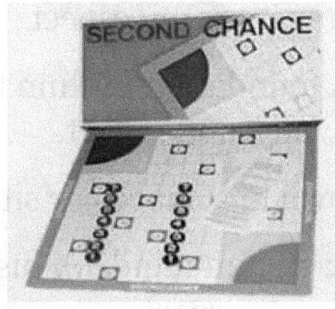

Cause now he was 21,
Reflect back

Raised by his mom
He was the only child
4 years old, smart enough to answer the phone
And sometimes he could dial

At 5, he wined, and fell out to get his own

You know how we do our little kids, say they bad and then say

They act so grown

And by 7

Never was taught rules and never was taught manners or respect

Or chores or a foundation for him to look back on a and reflect.

Like sitting down in a church or sitting in a car

And if you made him mind, oh just hear him roar!

And by 10, he was the boss of his momma's house

He was the cat and she was the mouse.

Never went to church and never was taught to pray

Reminds me of some parents I know today

By 15, he was stealing and running with a gang,

He was so bad in school and in the streets

They decided to change his name

Young Loc was more appealing

Than Kevin James Alton

Cause now he was dealing

In the streets he was balling

And we all know the path, the story ain't never changed

It's usually a dead end street, this is the drug game.

But on a Saturday night while riding through town with his boys

The driver stops for a drink and bamm, Ray

(In the back seat)

He heard a noise

And the next part is sad, cause it didn't have to happen

Life and its troubles will destroy you if you're found sleeping or napping.

Listening to the wrong people

Disregarding what Momma and Daddy said

Can get you arrested, hurt or even dead

And the truth gotta be told.

It never tarnishes, rots, or gathers dust, never grows old

But he was sitting in the back and never was supposed to be

Caught up in the crime

Funny how we can be in the wrong place at the wrong time.

Now a man has lost his life

Cause someone wanted to play God

Senseless violence is so cold and so hard.

Now all four are at the station, for one person's crime

Funny how trouble can take you farther than you want to go and make you pay more than you ever desired to pay.

Now his friends spread out in rooms, they trying to get a confession to this murder

You know when they call Ma, the news will surely hurt her

But the stories match up and to the driver, he'll reap what he sowed

Sometimes life isn't fair, but sometimes the guilty get punished.

In hard times or good

You gotta play with the cards you're furnished

Like Momma said…you can't do wrong and get by…

Strange how some of our young people and many of our old keep trying to try

So what about Ray, I know that's the question you desire to ask?

He goes to juvenile and gets 6 month probation, dirties his unblemished past

But that's a 2nd chance, I wonder if he'll it to his favor?

To succeed you must be perseverant

Lean but never waver.

And people deserve 2nd chances

And people deserve 2nd chances

Don't they?

Surprise Hug?

37 seconds of Power

I was just in Walmart buying some car cleaner. She came by exiting the door coming from some registers down the row walking with a woman.

I waved at her and said, HI.

Oh, I knew her for sure, but not close.

She smiled when she saw me and came toward me.

Why? I don't know, I'm not close to her.

She rarely speaks when I say hello.

She left her friend and gave me a big, tight hug.

I was speechless.

She has never hugged me in the 20 years I've known her.

Strange, maybe she needed a hug.

I asked the checkout lady. Why?

She said. ..Christmas spirit!!!!

I said no....

Love is 365...never 1 day. Sometimes people need a hug.

Listening is Vital

It was a 4 am Saturday morning, and we had planned a Houston trip to visit my family and attend a family gathering. It was my wife and I, and teenage kids who were all excited about getting out of town seeing something different.

I was driving and had my snacks and music to occupy me on this long, dark trip. As we got into Houston, we switched drivers, because I was now tired.

We had just entered Brazoria County and nearing the first town in my county, Pearland, when I asked if she'd like to stop at the upcoming Walmart. My wife said yes, because she needed some cosmetics, a snack, and some clothing items.

As we entered the parking lot she was looking for a parking spot right in front of the store. I immediately told her that this would be difficult, because people love to clog up the close spots. She likes to park right in front like most people, but there's nothing wrong with walking; it's good for you.

She insisted and angled to circle for that one good parking spot. I reiterated, just park toward the side and we'll find a good spot; people don't consider that idea.

She listened reluctantly and we found a very good spot a very short distance from the store. I opened the door, then she gathered her stuff and opened the door.

She looked down as she took a step down and saw it. Money balled up right at her foot. It was rolled up and there was no way she could avoid or miss it. $40, a blessing for a Saturday morning.

In life sometimes God uses others to bless you and allow you to see something that you're reluctant or unable to see. It's important that we recognize this as we help people break free from life's chains.

Listening is vital.

An open mind opens doors that were previously closed to us.

(Memorial to Renee)

Four months after I retired from Longview ISD in 2012, I started a part time job at the Paula Marin Jones Recreation on September 28.

2 days after I started, they hired another Recreational Clerk, Renee Clark to perform some of the feminine duties of the center.

For 2 years we had good times on holidays, birthday's daily work and laughs, and just enjoying the varied people who worked out there. Renee left in 2014, after finding new employment in the county. On August 1, 2016 after a battle with cancer, Renee joined the Lord

On my birthday. I miss her charm, talks, fellowships, just being herself and her love for the Dallas Cowboys.

This poetic piece is dedicated to Renee and the days we shared. It's also a tribute to all those who are dealing with

cancer, loved ones who've had cancer and an offerance of hope.

Just Renee

Even though I only worked with her about 2 years, I've grown to think a lot of her and learn from her.

She would slowly stroll in about 1 , packing every bag filled with chips, maybe a burger and various fruity things to snack on....and sometimes

I'd help her open the door, cause she forgot she only had 2 hands.

Just Renee

And as soon as she started to work, she needed to know every new thing that happened, was gonna happen, or needed to happen. She was inquisitive about the job, you tell her all, then she'd want to know more,, and then she'd go do some work.

Just Renee

Sometimes she'd call and say, I'm 5 minutes away do you need something from KFC or 5 Guys or some other restaurant…, but I knew

she was at least 15 minutes away. I'd stall for her. Oh and she had the coupons. And knew how to shop…..

She's get 20 %, 30 % off or buy 1 get one free on a pair of shoes. She saved me some money, cause I never knew about the sales she knew of…..

And we had our spats, but they only lasted about an hour or a day and then she'd be happy again or hug you

or do something small, but sweet for you and you knew she knew you didn't mean it.

It was Just Renee

I miss the holiday gatherings and birthday gatherings cause we had that in common, we loved to eat....

She'd make a list and tell everyone what to bring and sometimes where to get it and spread it from the clerks to the life guard,

And when it seemed like it wasn't going to be enough food, it was always too much.

She was a planner, always thinking, always give you a smile, but she could also give you that smirk.

She left the job and all the food gatherings, and the little comradery seemed to vanish,

And I started taking ugly pictures again...

And she knew how to take the best photos...

So I gotta close, but to the family she was a people person and loved her recreation center members, and they loved her.

I'll miss her, but I valued her, cause she was someone that no matter what, you learned to love and appreciate her.

One thing I remember was that she came one Monday and brought me and her a bible study book, She said, Terrell we gonna learn the bible together and share and have our own bible class.

I still have that book, I saw it the other day and I will start studying it as I remember Renee and what she meant to me and so many people.

Her love for Joe, Dillon, the Dallas Cowboys and just people will always be....

I wish more people had her qualities...

She was

Just Renee

8 Laws of Health

(New Start)

Chapter 14

Some things you learn in life through trial and error and as you know better, you do better.

One of the most remarkable things I have ever been exposed to I learned in 2016. It was learned from a friend, whom I considered an amazing person

full of biblical knowledge and genuineness.

The concepts she exposed me to will help not only balance my life, but set a tone to help others in life balancing.

The information is called the 8 laws of health. 8 components of life which operate to satisfy a person's spiritual, physical, and mental requirements.

They form an anachronism which spell out the letters:

NEW START

NUTRITION   EXERCISE   WATER

SUNSHINE TEMPERANCE AIR REST TRUST IN GOD

I'LL ESPOUND ON THESE 8 IN THE NEXT FEW PARAGRAPHS.

They begin with:

N Nutrition.....we are what we eat and our complex bodies require varied nutrients to fulfill daily performance needs.

E Exercise is vital and needed daily to keep bodily systems active.

W Water is important because our bodies *are 70 % water* and we need it for digestion, cell growth and production.

S Sunshine provides vitamin D and other minerals our bodies require.

T   Temperance relates to keeping our stress levels down each day.

A   Air invigorates the heart, lunch, brain and systems.

R Rest the body has to recover so **8ish hours** each night allots for that.

T Trust in God   6:33 I've learn to increase fruits and vegetables in my diet and blend in the colors of the food rainbow.

White strengthens the immune system.

Yellow promotes cell growth and allow our muscles, tissues and glands to perform better.

Orange nutrients are cancer protectors and fighters.

Brown foods lower the cholesterol and aid the heart systems.

Green foods detox the body and promote digestion.

Red foods aid the heart and the cardiovascular system.

Purple foods promote longer life.

    Seek ye first the kingdom of God and all his righteousness.

The 8 laws of health operate to create a framework to bring us a balances life.

37 Seconds to Impact

Questions and Answers

Chapter 15

 # 1 Joe .. African-American male, 31 years old, newly married , loves sports, Accountant, lives in Dallas, raised by father and mother

 # 2 Mary ...(70 year old retired, female, married, retired teacher, Christian mother)

 # 3 Robert.....56, white color worker, married with kids.

1. **How do you look at death?**

 # 1   Joe....Death is an end to life and this physical body but it's also a beginning to a new life.

#2 Mary....*Death is coming, because Jesus said, be ye also ready. Jesus went through too much for us to be saved and that any man should lose his life. Be ready for its coming.*

 # 3 Robert...I look at death as a reality, it's gonna occur as sure as we're born, we gonna die! We must respect that and be prepared on earth and most importantly be right with Jesus.

2.   Have you ever done anything for a homeless person? Why?

#1 Joe...*Yes, but you never really know who is homeless these days. I sometime don't trust people begging for money, because they may have a house, car, or be wanting drugs or alcohol. I did help a guy one time at a gas station, but I talked to him or a little bit and then gave him $ 2.*

#2 Mary.....*Yes, I've helped a homeless person before, but it was a group of people. I helped by way of a homeless mission, not on the street. It was an outreach help of clothes, food, money.*

 # 3 Robert.......*I've volunteered at a homeless mission and helped several homeless on the street; although I'm skeptical about giving money on the street; unless God led.*

3. Do you know any family member is an alcoholic? How could you help them get on track?

1 Joe.....Yes, I know one. I would let them spend time with me and show them that you can be more productive in life besides drinking.

#2 Mary......yes, I know some alcoholics and those in drug abuse also. Too help them you have to basically talk to them, but if they don't have a realization of their problem; there's little *you can do. You pray for them and pray God opens their heart to see their need.*

Yes, probably 3 people, but family think it's just a normal thing. I want to help them and feel they will hurt themselves or other, but unless they get out of denial; it's worthless. I pray for them and talk to them, but know they gotta be ready.

4. What is a millennial? How can you encourage them?

 # 1 Joe......*Those people in their 30's or people who become Adults after the year 2,000 or later. In high 1999 or later. I can encourage them by telling them to not be afraid to break away from their parents' beliefs. See the world and think from a different perspective. Use the internet for good and to don't think from a small perspective.*

#2 Mary.......*A Millennium is 1,000 years. It refers to Christ binding the devil for 1,000 years ,then after that he will be set loose to plunder in" Millennials".*

#3 Robert....*Someone born after 1996, between the ages of 22-36ish. They are more computer savvy, internet knowledgeable and values different from their parents.*

5. Some people are merely surviving, how can you teach them how to live?

 # 1 Joe....I would take a Shawshank quote..." Get busy or get busy dying". Set a purpose for everything you do. Connect everything you and makes sure there's a reason for all you do.

#3 Robert.....*There's only living in Christ, because he is the way, the truth, and the life. Go to God, ask him to rearrange your life.*

 # 2 Mary......*Evidently they have the wrong understanding of life if they are just surviving. Life is more abundantly lived. Spending more that you make creates stress and confusion in life. They need to rethink and reevaluate .*

their values that got them in trouble. What do they value? Lay up your treasures in heaven where neither dust nor other can rot it. I'd talk to them and pray for them if there'll listen.

6. What is a positive quote you live by that can help someone else?

#1 Joe......"I'm smart, and I'm handsome, but I don't know everything"

#2 Mary......What comes to my mind first is 23rd Psalms, the Lord is my shepherd I shall not want. God knows and can supply what you need and what you want. Remember that positive thoughts come from God and negative thoughts come from Satan. God is not into negativity. The devil comes for 3 reasons: to kill, steal and destroy. Trust in him and pray.

 # 3 Robert....." Free People '. You can't catch no fish, watching my pole. You gotta live your life.

6. Is 37 seconds a long time?

What can you do for someone in 37 seconds?

 # 1 Joe....37 seconds is a long time or short time depending on your perspective. If you are Usain Bolt running a 100 meter, then 37 seconds is a long time. If you are someone on their deathbed, then 37 seconds is short.

*To help someone in 37 seconds I would give them positive words, words with genuine meaning. Nonverbal communication speaks **louder at time than verbal.***

#2 Mary......I would trust the Lord and ask him what to say. I'd ask, are you saved? I'd ask if I could pray with them. No matter how I feel about it, I'd ask the Lord to lead me in it. No matter how they feel.

 # 3 Robert.....It's not quantity, its quality.

Prayer would be a factor that needs to be considered. Sometimes simply listening would be most valuable tool for reaching people.

37 SECONDS TO IMPACT

37 SECOND IMPACT STATEMENT..." We were all created for a purpose, by you understanding that your existence is not an accident. Also if you feel that alcohol, drugs, sex, whatever eases your pain, whatever you may do, or whatever to ease whatever you're going through is not it. So therefore

You have to consider and try to figure out now what is your purpose. The greater your battle is, the higher your calling may be. So you're here to help someone else.

So what are you gonna do? Are you gonna take your life or or you gonna help somebody else. Are you gonna quit or keep going?

Letter from my Grandmother to me on my birthday

August, 1985

(8 years before her death)

You'll never know how often

Those who love you say

" I wonder how he is

And you'll never know how often

Those who love you

Think of you

And wish you all
The very best
In everything you do

HAPPY BIRTHDAY
WITH LOVE

From
Carrie B. Edwards

It's the Little Things That Make the Difference

www.ingramcontent.com/pod-product-compliance
Lightning Source LLC
Chambersburg PA
CBHW051835090426
42736CB00011B/1822